Dto 10/1

# THE
# PRESENTATIONS
# POCKETBOOK

## By John Townsend
*Drawings by Phil Hailstone*

"Part of every Team Training Manager's presentation kit."
**Dr Hubert Konig, Managing Director, Team Training
International, Austria**

"This book has helped me, as a working manager, to
become an effective and self-confident business presenter."
**Graeme Cooper, Course Director, ABIN Bank Training
Institute, Germa**

*Many thanks to*

**Richard Bradley**

*for helping these*

*tips and*

*techniques*

*come alive in the*

*Powerful*

*Presentations'*

*workshop at the*

*Master Trainer*

*Institute.*

*Published by:*
**Management Pocketbooks Ltd**
Laurel House, Station Approach, Alresford, Hants SO24 9JH, U.K.
Tel: +44 (0)1962 735573   Fax: +44 (0)1962 733637
E-mail: sales@pocketbook.co.uk
Website: www.pocketbook.co.uk

As The Business Presenter's Pocketbook, first published in 1985 with later editions in 1993 and 1997.

Re-titled The Presentations Pocketbook, first published 2004. This edition published 2009

© John Townsend 1985, 1997, 2004, 2009.

British Library Cataloguing-in-Publication Data – A catalogue record for this book is available from the British Library.

ISBN 978 1 906610 15 9

Design, typesetting and graphics by **efex ltd**. Printed in U.K.

# CONTENTS

# INTRODUCTION

INTRODUCTION

# THE GREAT PRESENTATION SCANDAL

Every year millions of wasted hours are spent giving and attending business presentations. Why wasted? Because most presenters haven't asked why, what or who. It's a downright scandal!

And the problem is, they get away with getting it wrong. All over the world it seems that corporate ritual calls blindly for speakers to stand up beside a laptop and bore the pants off passive audiences!

Very few of them have the insight (or is it the courage?) to sit down before they start to plan a presentation and ask, 'Why have I been asked to speak; what's my message and who will be in the audience?'.

The result? Millions of hours of useless, droning, self-justifying speeches – and audiences who should be concerned, involved, motivated, simply blocking out the speakers and musing absent-mindedly until coffee or lunch.

# THE BEST

Just think back to the best presentation you've attended in the last couple of years.

Why was it so good?  What was the speaker's key message?  How was the presentation structured? How were the audio-visuals (if any)? What did the speaker do to grab your attention and keep it? Was it your frame of mind that allowed you to enjoy it?

The answer to all of these questions will point you to some basic principles of making a good presentation – identifying the key message, and then structuring, delivering and supporting it in a way that appeals to the audience so that they will remember it. As they say, the last born speaker died last week so we're on our own!

# THE PRESENTATION PARADOX

Do you know anyone who was fired for making a good presentation? I don't. Why, then, do so many people make boring presentations?

I think maybe they believe that to do it any other way would be rocking the boat. They would be seen as shallow, clownish and unprofessional – the first step to getting fired!

Isn't this a paradox?

Like in many sports, making a good presentation means facing up to the fear of failure. If you're skiing or snowboarding you have to point downhill and go for it. In windsurfing you have to lean back into the waves and in car rallies you have to steer into the skid.

Any bar pianist anywhere in the world will tell you that the most requested tune is Frank Sinatra's (I did it) 'My Way'. The problem is that most presenters will find that when the end is nigh and they face the final curtain – they didn't!

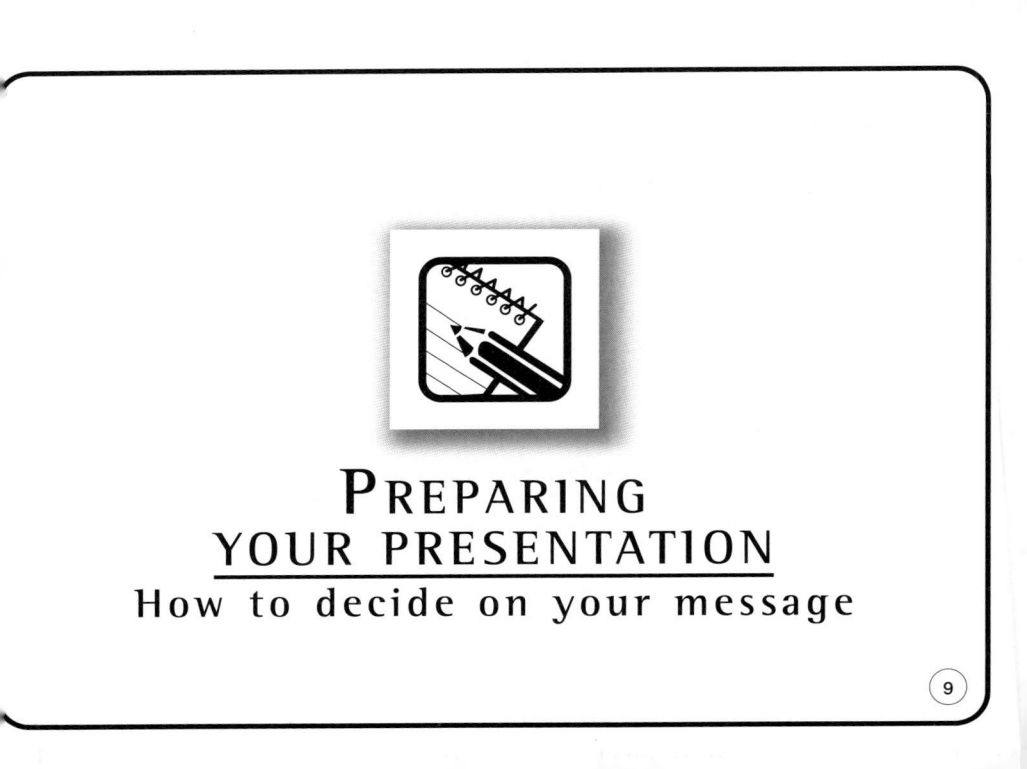

# PREPARING
## YOUR PRESENTATION
### How to decide on your message

## PREPARING YOUR PRESENTATION

# THE 3 W's
WHY?

'A wise man asks himself seven times 'why?' before acting.'

- Why am I going to give this presentation?
  - To provide information?
  - To represent my function?
  - To entertain?
  - To fill up the agenda?
  - To sell my ideas?
  - To defend a position?
  - To be provocative?

# THE 3 W's

## WHY?

- Whatever the answer, keep asking 'why?' in other ways ...
    - What is the objective I wish to achieve?
    - What is happening **now** that I wish to change or clarify?
    - What will I accept as evidence that my speech has succeeded?
    - What must the audience do or think at the end?

    ... until it becomes obvious **what** your essential messages must be.

## PREPARING YOUR PRESENTATION

# THE 3 W's
## WHAT? (THE MESSAGE)

Answering the question 'why?' properly will tell you **what** your key message should be

- If it is to make a budget proposal then SELL your ideas, concentrating on the benefits rather than the details of your project
- If it is to provide information, select only the 'MUST knows' and keep the 'NICE TO knows' for a hand-out or face-to-face
- If it is to wake people up or entertain, keep content low and concentrate on interest, humour or audio-visual devices

**Remember!**
All the research (as well as YOUR experience) shows that, however intelligent your audience is, they will neither want, nor be able to absorb, more than four or five key messages.

## PREPARING YOUR PRESENTATION

# THE 3 W's
## WHAT? (THE VEHICLE)

A vehicle is a mechanism which encapsulates your message in an interesting format so that it's easy to follow and remember. It's a device for 'carrying' your message to the audience. Technically speaking, a vehicle will ensure that the message will be understood by the right brain as well as the left brain and, therefore, make it twice as powerful.

Vehicles come in many forms. Here are just a few:

- A metaphor or analogy. Every time you say, 'It's a bit like…' and compare your system/department to something less technical, people sit up, open their eyes and …listen!

- A mnemonic device. Acronyms like PAMPERS and FLICK (pages 38/54) are simple ways of packaging messages but there are many more

- Alliterations help make dull sequences lively

- Slogans, theme tunes, logos and mascots will illustrate your message and make it unforgettable

- Devices like jigsaws or bricks can help 'build' messages

- Props, gadgets and gimmicks to see, hear or touch add interest through involvement

# PREPARING YOUR PRESENTATION

## THE 3 W's

### WHO? (THE AUDIENCE)

Once you know exactly **why** you are going to make the presentation and **what** your key points will be, you must ask, **'Who will be in the audience?'** – so as to customise your message and make it stick.

- Who are the participants? Level? Background?
- What do they already know about the subject?
- Are they really interested? (If not, I'll have to create the interest)
- What are their **WIFT**'s? (**W**hat's **I**n it **F**or **T**hem?)
- How fast can they absorb what I'm saying?
- What do they **expect** me to say?
- What are their mind-sets?
  (prejudices, attitudes, beliefs etc)

**Tip** *To be sure you have tailored your speech to the audience, play devil's advocate and ask, 'How could I best offend them if I really wanted to?!'*

# THE FIGURE FALLACY

A lot of people seem to believe that to be credible you have to fill up slide after slide with figures and that if something is serious then it has to be painful.

Again, think back to the presentations you remember and enjoyed. They probably didn't resemble a doctorial thesis, nor was the speaker trying to win the Nobel Prize for technical accuracy. You have forgotten all those speakers who suffered 'analysis paralysis' and remember only those who had a useful message for you, or who were lively, interesting and professional.

# EXAMPLE

One of the best presentations I ever attended was given by a dour Scotsman, general manager of a subsidiary of a large multinational. He opened by saying he'd been asked to give a presentation wearing a kilt but could not afford to buy one. Nor could the company afford to buy him one, in light of the cost-cutting programme which had led to the successful year he was about to describe to us. This brought howls of laughter because we all knew he wasn't joking!

In his 15-minute presentation (he was scheduled for 40 on the agenda) he showed three slides, each with one huge figure on it.

Each figure was one of his company's objectives set the previous year.

He told us why he'd chosen these and bet us that we hadn't remembered them from his last year's boring presentation.

**He was right!**

He then described some of the universally applicable methods he and his company had used to meet these objectives. I remember a couple of the tips to this day!

# STRUCTURING
## YOUR PRESENTATION
### How to package your message

# BIKER 'B'

## STRUCTURING YOUR PRESENTATION

## BIKER 'B'

A mnemonic device to help you structure your presentation so that it will carry your message to the audience!

| | |
|---|---|
| **B**ang! | Always start with an attention-getting 'hook' which suits your personality and topic |
| **I**ntroduction | Outline the key points of your message (route map) and introduce your 'vehicle' |
| **K**ey points | Present 1-5 key points (maximum) using your vehicle – WIFT (What's In it For Them?) |
| **E**xamples | Give at least one example per key point to link to participants' experience and help them remember |
| **R**ecap | Go over the key points again and summarise 'take-aways' |
| **B**ang! | Always finish with a closing 'hook' – if possible linked to the opening bang |

# THE OPENING **B**ANG

You don't have to be a clown to start your presentation with a bang.

All professional communicators do it. Watch any TV documentary. Read any newspaper or magazine article. Listen to any good speech or radio show.

Remember, your audience has almost always something better to do with their mind than listen to you!

Starting with a bang **which suits your personality and your subject** will demonstrate to the audience that you value their attention and that your respect them enough to make your presentation **relevant, interesting and professional**.

# 5 TYPES OF **B**ANG

 **THE CLASSICAL BANG**
Introduce your presentation with one or two punchy highlights ('This presentation could save you four million Euros!')

**THE 'IMAGINE' BANG**
- Appeal to a common memory ('You may all remember when…')
- Evoke a hypothetical situation ('Imagine that…')
- Create a metaphor ('Imagine that my ABC system is a bit like…')
- Tell a relevant parable ('Once upon a time…')

**THE MYSTERY BANG**
Disguise your opening with 2-3 ambiguous clues to your message

**THE PARTICPATION BANG**
- Ask a question
- Ask for a volunteer to do or say something

**THE DRAMATIC BANG**
- Use a gimmick/accessory
- Use surprise visual/sketch
- Make a provocative statement
- Tell a humorous story (no jokes!)

# Introduction

There is a famous saying about making good presentations which goes:

*Tell 'em what you're going to tell 'em. Tell 'em and, then, tell 'em what you've told 'em!*

The introduction is where you *tell 'em what you are going to tell 'em*. In order to follow the key points on your message 'trip', the audience will need a route map. Give them a succinct outline of your main points so they can relax and enjoy the journey.

# **K**EY POINTS

This is where you *tell 'em!*

- Restrict your message to 1-5 key points. If you find this difficult, it's probably because you haven't asked enough 'why's'

- Ask yourself WIFT – What's In it For Them?

- When in doubt, cut it out!

- Include only key points which support your main message and think, 'What would I need to hear if I were in their shoes?'

**ABOVE ALL**
- Work on your vehicle! An elegant presentation is one where the key points are honed and pared to the minimum, where the vehicle is powerful and clear, and where the 'take-aways' or deliverables are concise and obvious to all

# EXAMPLES

Hand-in-hand with the need to link your key points to the participants' needs and experience goes the need to give examples.

Apart from a few real theorists, people need to be able to visualise, or feel your message. Just think back to when something someone was explaining to you suddenly became clear when they gave you an example.

For each of your 1-5 key points be sure to give an example, show an illustration, or tell a story which DEMONSTRATES what you're trying to put across.

**NB** *If you've created a good vehicle this in itself will represent the examples – or at least help you to find some.*

# Recap

This is where you *tell 'em what you told 'em!*

If you think about it, just about every professional communication finishes with a recap or a quick summary. Our brains need a recap if we are to remember the key points ('Here are the news headlines again…').

By making a recap you help the audience by handing them their 'take-aways' on a plate. You may even want to summarise your key points on a handout and distribute them.

If you fail to recap, you jeopardise the retention in the audience's memory of your message. Be warned!

# THE FINAL **B**ANG

Most presentations end not with a bang, but with mumbled requests for questions, apologies or other whimpers. Do yourself a favour and:

**Always finish with a BANG!**

- A statement which dramatically sums up your key message
- A visual or verbal link back to your opening bang
- An unexpected action, happening or apparition
- Simply a determined, 'Thank you for your attention' (always 'ask' for applause even if you won't get it)

*Imagine* ... that each presentation is a gift for the audience. If the 'vehicle' and the structure are the wrapping, the ending bang is the ribbon!

## QUESTIONS ABOUT QUESTIONS

Many presenters think that the best way to end a presentation is with a Q & A (Question and Answer) session. When the audience is small and the topic touches peoples' lives and work then these sessions can be effective – even essential. However, with bigger audiences and more formal sessions, think about the following points:

● Experience shows that most participants are too shy to ask a genuine question in front of so many people. Those who request the spotlight, therefore, rarely ask a real question. Their motivation is often to:

    - score points with colleagues or bosses

    - air grievances or push an embarrassing point which would have been more effectively handled face-to-face

    - 'hi-jack' the attention of the audience on to one of their pet subjects

## QUESTIONS ABOUT QUESTIONS (Cont'd)

- In large meeting rooms many participants can't even hear the question (don't care or would rather be playing golf). By the time the roving microphone gets there, the speaker is halfway through the answer! Having shouted 'speak up' once or twice, the others give up and slip back into reverie

- If there is an issue which you have not covered, it is probably confidential or you are unprepared. In both cases, probing questions will force you to hedge, defend or, at best, say you cannot answer

So… why ask for questions?

## TIMING

Remember the 50% rule:

**Rehearse it.  Time it.  Cut it by 50%.**
This will ensure that you allow for:

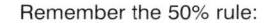

- A late start
- An over-run by previous speaker
- Sharing passing thoughts triggered by the environment
- Participants' questions etc

**Always** stick to the schedule – whatever the consequences. Over-running on a presentation is **always** bad because:

- The senior participants will conclude that you can't plan and will worry about the schedule – and your career!
- Your fellow speakers will resent you taking **their** time
- Non-speaking participants will stop listening and start thinking about coffee or lunch or their holiday in Spain

# NOTES

Once you've answered the 3 W's and decided on the structure of your presentation, you'll want to start making notes. But, however carefully you prepare yourself, experience has shown that, if you're like most speakers, you'll abandon your voluminous notes as soon as you hit the platform and rely on wordy, boring slides.

People like Tony Buzan have shown that **KEY WORDS** are all your brain needs to trigger back all the information you've prepared and that **DRAWINGS** and **LOGOS** are even more effective for recall.

You'll find that condensing your notes onto one **A6 CARD** like the example shown over the page is quite sufficient as a memory aid – and it leaves you free to use bold and simple slides and flip charts.

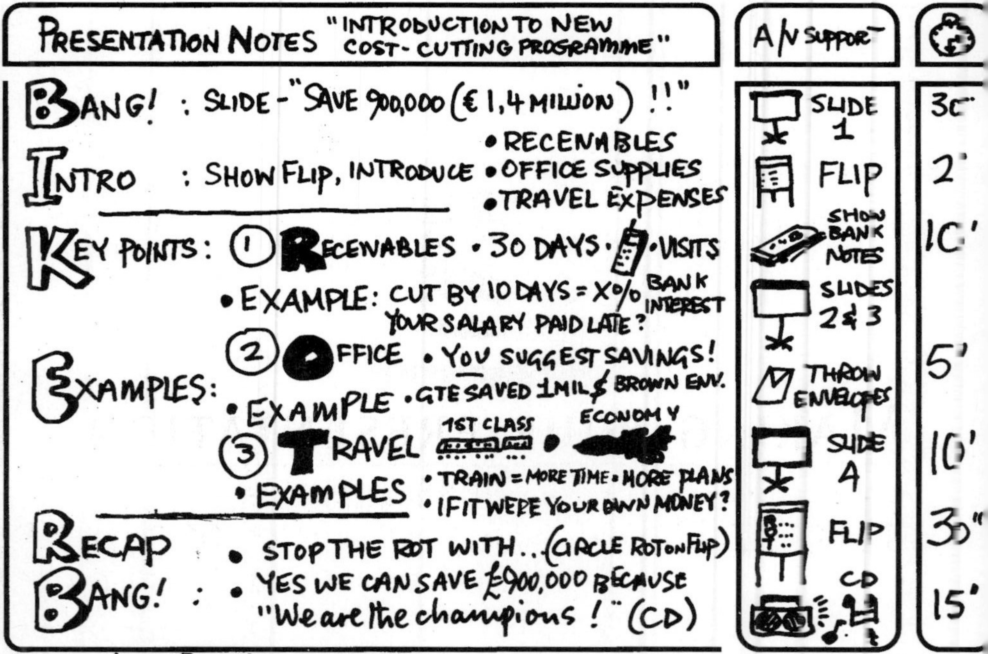


• See also "The Story of Max"

# MAKING YOUR PRESENTATION
How to get your message across and
feel at ease in front of an audience

MAKING YOUR PRESENTATION

# YOUR COMPETITION

## TV: THE 3 P's

Where have most of your participants seen most presentations since they left school or university? No, not in their organisation's conference room but in their living-room, in front of the TV. For just about everyone these days, television provides most of their mind-forming (and deforming) messages.

As presenters, therefore, our competition is not only from other presenters, but also from TV. Whether we like it or not, our participants are comparing us, consciously or unconsciously, to people they've seen on the box – the professional communicators. This competition comes in three forms. **The 3 P's: Publicity, Presenters and Performers.**

Can we compete? Can we reach this level of professionalism? Of course we can…and we must. But it means another 6 P's! Practise. Practise. Practise. Prepare. Prepare. Prepare.

The trouble is, you probably won't get fired by your organisation for being less professional than the TV presenters. But you will get zapped by the participants!

# YOUR COMPETITION

## TV PRESENTERS

Not all TV presenters are totally polished superstars with silver tongues. But they are professionals. They keep their jobs by being articulate, understandable and relatively interesting.

They are backed-up by invisible teams of professionals who provide a generally high level of audio-visual support. Their messages are, therefore, well-structured, colourful and succinct. They often appeal to all our senses and are frequently amusing. They are present in our participants' homes at the touch of a button and, if they fail to hold their attention, they are zapped with a jab of a finger.

# YOUR COMPETITION
## TV PUBLICITY

Consider the power and the punch of modern publicity editing. In the early days of television, cutting was slow and ponderous. A recent article in 'The Economist' reported that, in the eighties, sound and vision bites could be up to 15 seconds long (that's also what I was taught when learning to use my old movie camera). By 2000, TV advertising agencies were taking advantage of research into their viewers' attention and interest span, and had cut it down to images per second rather than seconds per clip! Just watch any TV adverts and count the cuts. Our participants are used to fast-moving consumer goods being sold by fast-moving messages!

# YOUR COMPETITION

## TV PERFORMERS

Whenever our participants' preferred TV station needs to get across a particularly important message, they call in the professional performers. These talented people use a whole array of skills to enchant their audiences, starting with the studied appearance and grooming. The practised timing of their delivery, their eye contact, the seeming ease with which they interact with the studio audience, the cameras or the guest speaker(s) – all provide an aura of confident professionalism.

# USING YOUR VOICE

**P**rojection     Speak louder than usual; throw your voice to back of room

**A**rticulation     Don't swallow words. Beware of verbal 'tics'

**M**odulation     Vary tone and pitch; be dramatic, confidential and/or triumphant

**P**ronunciation     Watch tonic accents; check difficult words; beware of malapropisms

**E**nunciation     Over emphasise. Accentuate syllables

**R**epetition     Repeat key phrases with different vocal emphasis

**S**peed     Use delivery speed to manipulate the audience; **fast** delivery to excite and stimulate; **slow** delivery to emphasise, inspire awe, dramatise and control

# NERVES: THE MURPHY MONKEY

As you get up to speak, it's as if a monkey has suddenly jumped onto your shoulders. He claws your neck and weighs you down – making your knees feel weak and shaky. As you start to speak, he pulls at your vocal chords and dries up your saliva. He pushes your eyes to the floor, makes your arms feel 10 metres long and attaches a piece of elastic to your belt – pulling you back to the table or wall behind you!

Experienced speakers know about the Murphy monkey. Within the first 30 seconds they throw him to the audience! When you throw the monkey to one of the participants, suddenly the spotlight is on them and not on you. How ...?

- A question, a show of hands, a short 'icebreaker' (participant introductions, an exercise or quiz etc) a discussion, a 'volunteer' or simply a reference to one or more of the participants – all these are ways of putting the monkey on their backs for a few moments

This takes the pressure off you and gives you time to relax, smile and get ready to communicate your message loud and clear.

# DRESS

- Avoid black and white and other strongly contrasting colours
- Wear comfortable, loose-fitting clothes
- If you can't make up your mind, wear something boring – at least your clothes won't detract from the message!
- Try and dress one step above the audience
- Check zips and buttons before standing up

# LIGHTHOUSE TECHNIQUE

Sweep the audience with your eyes, staying only 2-3 seconds on each person – unless in dialogue.

This will give each participant the impression that you are speaking to him/her personally and ensure attention, in the same way as the lighthouse keeps you awake by its regular sweeping flash of light. Above all, avoid looking at one (friendly-looking) member of the audience or at a fixed (non-threatening) point on the wall or floor.

# BODY LANGUAGE AND MANNERISMS

- Don't be tempted by manual props (pens, pointers, spectacles etc)
- Don't keep loose change in your pocket
- Be aware of your verbal 'tics' and work on eliminating them (eg 'OK!' – 'You know' – 'and so forth' – 'Now ...')
- Watch out for furniture!
- Avoid 'closed' or tense body positions
- Don't worry about pacing, leaning etc
- Check your hair/tie/trousers/dress before standing up!
- When you forget your body – so will they!

# FACILITATING DISCUSSION
## SOCRATIC DIRECTION

Take a tip from the Ancient Greeks.

If you wish to encourage audience participation to prove a point, use **Socratic Direction**.

**K** now the answers you want but know that you don't know everything!

**O** pen with open questions

**P** araphrase participants' answers

**S** ummarise contributions (flip chart?)

**A** dd your own points

(43)

# QUESTIONS AND INTERRUPTIONS

Most participant questions are not questions. They are requests for the spotlight. If it's one of those rare, closed **real** questions – answer it succinctly.

If not, first:

- **REFLECT** back to the questioner what you thought was the question

    ('If I understand correctly, you're asking ...')

Depending on how the questioner 'reformulates' the question, answer it, **OR**:

- **DEFLECT** it as follows:

    **Group** : 'How do the rest of the group feel?'

    : 'Has anyone else had a similar problem?'

    **Ricochet** : (to one participant) 'Bill, you're an expert on this. What do you think?'

    **Reverse** : (back to questioner) 'You've obviously done some thinking on this, what's **your** view?'

# DEALING WITH CHALLENGING PARTICIPANTS

1. **The Heckler**
- Probably insecure
- Gets satisfaction from needling
- Aggressive and argumentative

What to do:
- Never get upset
- Find merit, express agreement on **something**, move on
- Wait for a mis-statement of fact and then throw it out to the group for correction

# DEALING WITH CHALLENGING PARTICIPANTS

## 2. The Talker/Know All

- An 'eager beaver'/chatterbox
- A show-off
- Well-informed and anxious to show it

What to do:

- Wait until he/she takes a breath, thank, refocus and move on
- Slow him/her down with a tough question
- Jump in and ask group to comment
- Use as a 'co-presenter' – maybe he/she has some interesting points to add!

# DEALING WITH CHALLENGING PARTICIPANTS

### 3. The Griper

- Feels 'hard done by'
- Probably has a pet 'peeve'
- Will use you as scapegoat

What to do:

- Get him/her to be specific
- Show that the purpose of your presentation is to be positive and constructive
- Use peer pressure – ask group how they feel

# DEALING WITH CHALLENGING PARTICIPANTS

4. **The Whisperers** (There's only one; the other is the 'whisperee'!)

- Don't understand what's going on – clarifying or translating
- Sharing anecdotes triggered by your presentation
- Bored, mischievous or hypercritical (unusual)

What to do:

- Stop talking, wait for them to look up and 'non-verbally' ask for their permission to continue
- Use 'lighthouse' technique (see page 41)

# FOOD FOR THOUGHT
### DRIVERS AND PEDESTRIANS

- When we are **participants** at a presentation, we are like pedestrians who criticise road hogs – we complain about boring, long-winded speeches. Then, like drivers who ignore pedestrians, we get up to make **our** presentation and do exactly the same!

    So... think like a pedestrian!

## MAKING YOUR PRESENTATION

# TEN TIPS

- Don't keep your eyes on your notes
- Never read anything except quotations
- If you're not nervous there's something wrong
- Exaggerate body movements and verbal emphasis
- **Perform** (don't act);  perform = 'fournir' (to supply) and 'per' (for)
- Pause often – silence is much longer for **you** than for the audience
- Use humour; a laugh is worth a thousand frowns!
- Be enthusiastic; if you're not, why should they be?
- Don't try and win the Nobel prize for technical accuracy
- **KISS** – **K**eep **I**t **S**imple, **S**tupid!

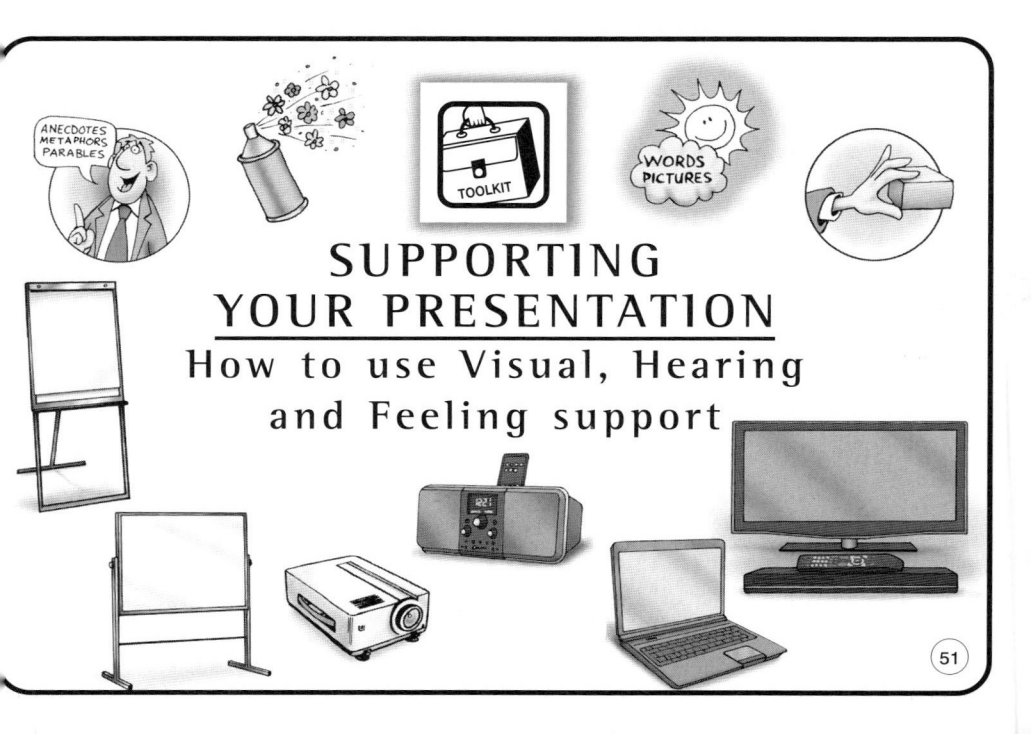

# SUPPORTING YOUR PRESENTATION
## How to use Visual, Hearing and Feeling support

## SUPPORTING YOUR PRESENTATION

# VHF COMMUNICATION

The human brain stores information in VHF – as Visual, Hearing or Feeling data.

Each participant has a preferred channel for remembering data. In my on-going classroom experiment on recall, 51% of participants say that their memory favours visual information, while only 7% prefer words/lectures and sounds. An astonishing 42% say they remember feelings, tastes, smells and tactile experiences best.

In order to 'tune in' to the maximum number of participants' wavelengths, professional speakers use a wide range of transmitters!

**V**
- Imaging ● Flip chart ● Pinboard ● Whiteboard ● Laptop ● Video projector
- PowerPoint slides ● Props and accessories ● Video/DVD clips ● Word pictures

**H**
- Music (instant access CDs or MP3 for changes of mood/illustrations)
- Sound effects ● Audio gimmicks ● Onomatopoeia

**F**
- Music (emotion/mood setting) ● Handouts ● Verbal descriptions
- Anecdotes ● Metaphors ● Parables ● Smells ● Tastes ● Cross-sensing

**Feelings stay longer than facts!**

# PRESENTATION EMERGENCY KIT

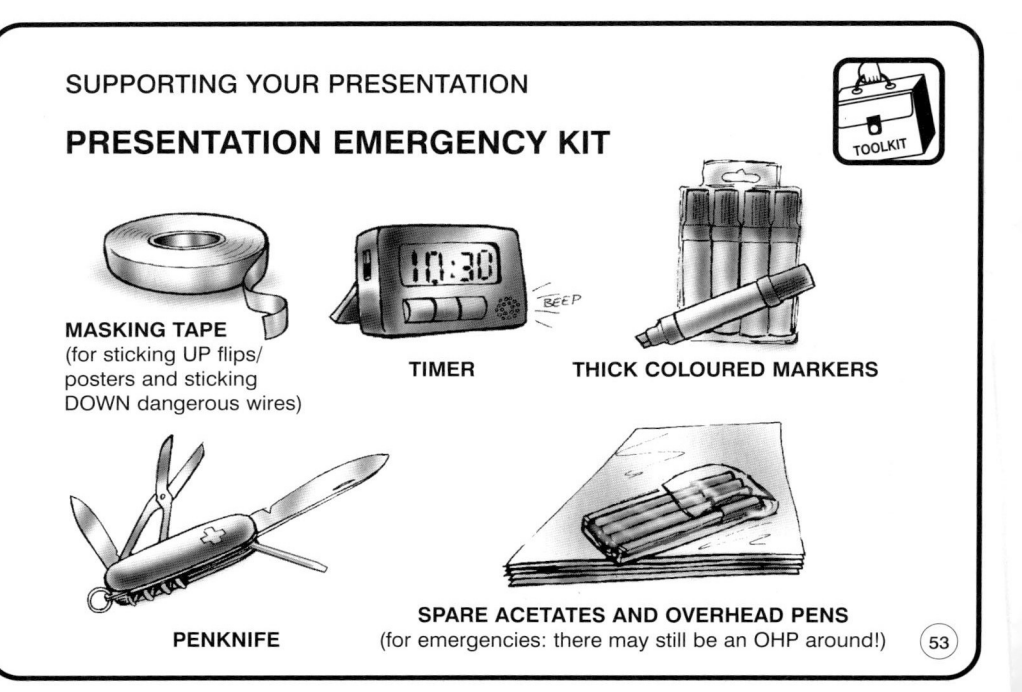

**MASKING TAPE**
(for sticking UP flips/
posters and sticking
DOWN dangerous wires)

**TIMER**

**THICK COLOURED MARKERS**

**PENKNIFE**

**SPARE ACETATES AND OVERHEAD PENS**
(for emergencies: there may still be an OHP around!)

(53)

## SUPPORTING YOUR PRESENTATION

# V : VISTIPS

## GOLDEN RULES FOR SLIDES & FLIP CHARTS

**Frame**
- Use a standard **frame** for all visuals
- Create a **logo** or numbering system

**Letters**
- Use **LARGE, LEGIBLE LETTERS**
- Legible from 10 metres!
- Text 30-50 pts (on PowerPoint slides)
- Titles 70-100 pts (on PowerPoint slides)

**Images**
- Use at least one **IMAGE/LOGO/GRAPH** on every visual

**Colour**
- Use at least **one colour** more than black on every visual

**Kiss**
- Keep it short and simple!
- 1 topic. Bullet points and key words
- Six lines maximum
- Six words per line maximum

# **V** : HEALTH WARNING!

## VISUAL VALIUM

Just about every visual aid I've ever seen during a management presentation seems to have been designed to send me to sleep – a kind of visual Valium.

Too many words; too busy; no attempt to use space properly; no images; little or no colour. After a couple, I simply can't keep my eyes open.

Unfortunately, with the advent of presentations software they've become worse! Now they are professionally bad! Despite what your corporate identity programme might say, even a well-designed information slide becomes sleep-inducing when the same design is used over and over for different messages.

## SUPPORTING YOUR PRESENTATION

# V : HEALTH WARNING!

At a recent conference I counted the words and/or numbers on every professional looking slide shown by every particularly unprofessional speaker!

For the 37 slides shown by one earnest presenter, the average per slide was 95 words or figures. The overall conference average was 76 words per slide.

And almost every speaker read almost every one of them! Some of them said, *'You can't read this but what it says is…'* and then proceeded to read them to us. Some just turned to the screen and read them. Some tried but couldn't read them, so we had to try on our own while they talked about something else!

# **V** : SLIDE TIPS

Use the 'storyboard' approach:

- One slide with **chapter headings**
- One slide **per** chapter heading with a summary of key points (3-5)
- One slide **per** point/topic in each chapter
- Print series name and number on each
- Concentrate message in centre
- Use only $^2/_3$ of space for message
- **Always** include at least one illustration

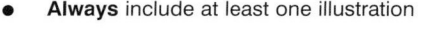

**NB**

USE THE **FLICK** VISTIPS STANDARD! (See page 54)

## SUPPORTING YOUR PRESENTATION

# V : SLIDE TIPS

### THE 3 BE'S

Just about **every** time you want, need or have to make a presentation, people won't want, need or have to know the whole story! Think about how **you** feel during other people's presentations. The art of good slide presentation can be summed up with the 3 Be's.

**BE BOLD** – Don't follow the crowd. Use colour and illustrations.
Take time to choose appropriate photos or clip art. WORDS ARE NOT VISUALS.
Use huge letters. Forget grammar!

**BE BRIEF** – Think about your topic. What's the real message?
Forget the detail; how can you reduce the number of slides to the bare minimum?

**BE SEATED!** – Try and finish before your allotted deadline.
Everyone will appreciate it – however important the message.

SUPPORTING YOUR PRESENTATION

# V : SLIDE TIPS

GRAPHIC/CLIP ART

- Example of a slide illustrating that wood burning stoves in Kenya save $25 million a year and help fight deforestation.

**$25,000,000**

# V : SLIDE TIPS

GRAPHIC/CLIP ART

- Example of a slide from a financial presentation, likening the function to a ship's sonar.

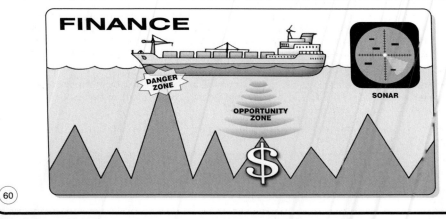

# V : SLIDE TIPS (POWERPOINT)

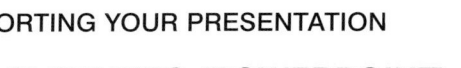

## ILLUSTRATIONS

### Clip Art

You can import any of your own pictures, photos, cartoons, drawings, etc into a PowerPoint presentation. If you're searching for something new or special (like the ship on the previous page) try looking in PowerPoint's Clip Art collection and cut and paste it onto a slide – either from the library or go on line and type in the name of the kind of illustration you need. Most of the time you'll find many different images to choose from.

### Animations

PowerPoint's 50 or so 'animations' can give any slide a video effect by moving text or pictures in and out of the screen in ever more ingenious ways. Just go to 'Custom Animation' and get clicking!

*Warning!* Don't overdo it. People are getting a bit fed up with text whizzing and scooting about just for the sake of it.

SUPPORTING YOUR PRESENTATION

# **V** : SLIDE TIPS (POWERPOINT)

VIDEO

There are basically three ways of showing video clips during your presentation:

- With a stand-alone video player/hard disk and TV screen
- By inserting a DVD in the hard disk drive of your laptop and playing it to the audience on a large screen with a video projector (it will play automatically using one of the media players installed on your computer)
- Embedding your video clips/film directly into your PowerPoint presentation. For this you'll need to copy your selected video piece onto the hard disk in an appropriate format for PowerPoint to recognise and then import it into the slide concerned through 'Insert' and then 'Movie' (2007 version)

(See also Page 75)

SUPPORTING YOUR PRESENTATION

# **V** : SLIDE TIPS (POWERPOINT)

SOUNDS

### PowerPoint sounds

There are 20 or so sounds available in PowerPoint's 'Custom Animation' which you can add to text or object movements. In the 2007 version there is also a whole range of effects from thunder to guitar or classical music available from the 'Insert' and 'Sounds' tabs.

### Linking or embedding your own music/sounds

You can create your own WAV or MP3 versions of music and other sound bites to insert into slides so that they will play as you click to the appropriate slide or continue to play across several slides.

For more information on embedding sounds and music go to
**www.presentationhelper.co.uk**

# V : SLIDE TIPS (POWERPOINT)

## PRINT SCREEN

A really simple way of getting web pages and other illustrations into your slides is to use the Print Screen feature on your computer.

Whatever you have on the screen at any time can be captured onto the clipboard and inserted into a PowerPoint slide by pressing the Print Screen/SysRq key on the keyboard, opening the slide to which you want to add what you've captured and then pressing Ctrl V – just like any cut and paste operation.

*Remember, though, that not all web pages make for easy reading on a small video projection screen at 10 metres!* (See pages 54 and 67).

Print Screen/SysRq

SUPPORTING YOUR PRESENTATION

# V : SLIDE TIPS
## LIVE WEB PAGES

In many conference rooms you can go online with your laptop, and project websites onto the large screen for all to see.

Going 'live' to a website during your presentation might be a real shortcut to your key message. Be careful though not to share all your click manoeuvres with the audience!

Set things up so that you can get to the page you want quickly. Black out the projector screen until you have the page ready to show and remember, the longer you take to get there, the more restless the audience will become.

A good website for how to link live web pages is **www.pptfaq.com**

SUPPORTING YOUR PRESENTATION

# V : SLIDE TIPS
## USING A WEBCAM

### Interviews, messages and demonstrations
Although it might seem a little complicated logistically, you could add a bit of topical interest to your presentation (as a stand alone visual aid or in between slides) by bringing an absent colleague or expert into the room for a live interview or a demonstration of something via webcam.

### Examples:
- A brief Q and A session with the HR director on a new policy
- An important message from the CEO
- A demo of a new product by a technical person
- An on-site report from a sales person
- A quick look at a new building with the facilities manager

**Tip** *Make sure you've briefed the 'on-camera' colleague to be prepared to wait on the line for you to go live and, when the moment comes, try to make the link, from what you're saying to the live webcam picture, seamless. Murphy's Law is particularly applicable to this process!*

## SUPPORTING YOUR PRESENTATION

# V : SLIDE TIPS

## DANGERS: DO'S AND DON'TS

### DO

✔ Remember the **FLICK** Golden Rules from page 54

✔ Bear in mind that just because something is technically clever or easy to access doesn't necessarily make it good visually

✔ Beware of 'blinding them with science'...I've seen potentially great presentations ruined by technical overkill or collapse (sometimes literally) into the arms of Murphy

✔ **KISAP** (KEEP IT SIMPLE AND PUNCHY)

### DON'T

✘ Share your keyboard prowess with the group. The audience are not gathered around your desk peeking over your shoulder as you surf the ether, they are spending their valuable time at a meeting or conference and expecting a professional presentation not a demonstration of computer skills

✘ Forget to **KISAP**!

# V : THE FLIP CHART

Despite (or maybe because of) the advent of hi-tech, all singing, all dancing PowerPoint software, the good old three-legged faithful friend, the flip chart is **increasing** in popularity with presenters in front of small- to medium-sized audiences.

## Why?

- Portable (unlike most projection screens)
- Can be pre-prepared
- Intimate and less formal
- Generative – can be created on the spot, especially with audience input
- FRIENDLY!

# V : FLIP TIPS

### PREPARATION

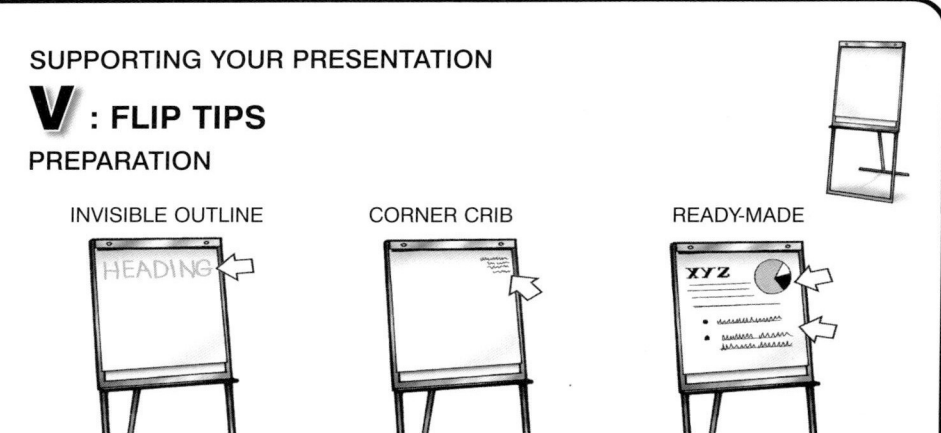

INVISIBLE OUTLINE

Lightly pencil in headings in advance when unsure of space, drawing, handwriting etc

CORNER CRIB

Use the top corner to pencil in your notes for each chart. Write small and no one will notice!

READY-MADE

Prepare key charts in advance

## SUPPORTING YOUR PRESENTATION

# V : FLIP TIPS

## GRAPHICS

### **A**TTRACTIVE
- Give each flip a title
- Use bullet points (like the ones on this page)
- Use at least two dark colours

### **B**IG & BOLD
- Use **thick** markers (bring your own!)
- Should be legible from 10 metres!

### **C**APITAL KEY WORDS
- Never write sentences!

# V : FLIP TIPS

## GRAPHICS

Whenever possible, use **cartoons** or **drawings** to personalise and add interest to your headings.

# V : FLIP TIPS

## GRAPHICS

### Standing

Every time you turn your back on the audience
your voice and their attention disappear.

Since you can't write and face the
audience at the same time (unless
you are a contortionist!)
you should:

- Write (a few words/seconds)
- Turn and talk
- Write (a few words/seconds)
- Turn and talk

# V : GRAPHICS

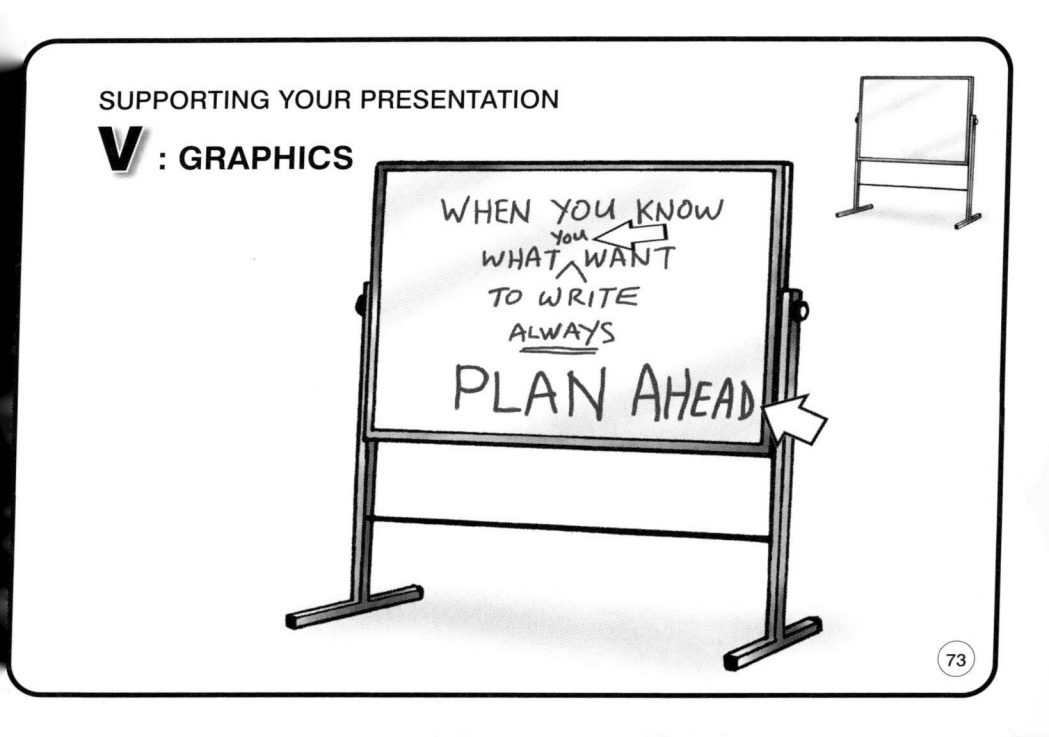

## SUPPORTING YOUR PRESENTATION

# V : THE WHITEBOARD

## WRITING AND STICKING

**Write on!**
- Replaces blackboard (school memories)
- Great for brainstorming
- Change colour often
- Only use appropriate whiteboard pens

**Stick up!**
- Use 'Post-it' stickers to create group-work summaries (key phrases only); stick on whiteboard
- Move stickers into columns or categories; use pens to draw bubbles round salient groupings or to make links between stickers

## SUPPORTING YOUR PRESENTATION

# V : VIDEO

In today's multi-media world, video is a virtually indispensable tool for professional presenters. Here are some advantages and disadvantages of using video:

- Professional, fast-moving
- In tune with participants' background/expectations
- Can be inserted into a PowerPoint presentation

<br/>

- Few videos give **exactly** the message you want
- Expensive to buy/hire/download
- Technically subject to Murphy's Law

*Create your own video clips or edit others on the computer.*
*They may not be totally professional but they will be unique!*

# V : THE TALKING WALL

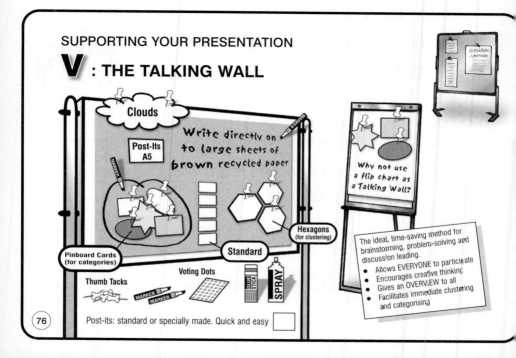

Clouds

Post-Its
A5

Write directly on
to large sheets of
brown recycled paper

Pinboard Cards
(for categories)

Standard

Hexagons
(for clustering)

Why not use
a flip chart as
a Talking Wall?

The ideal, time-saving method for
brainstorming, problem-solving and
discussion leading.
- Allows EVERYONE to participate
- Encourages creative thinking
- Gives an OVERVIEW to all
- Facilitates immediate clustering
  and categorising

Thumb Tacks

Voting Dots

GLUE STICK

SPRAY

76

Post-its: standard or specially made. Quick and easy

SUPPORTING YOUR PRESENTATION

# H : USING MUSIC AND SOUND EFFECTS

Here are some ways you should be using recorded music in your presentation:

- To create a friendly atmosphere at the beginning of the presentation as participants come in, meet each other and settle down
- As background music during coffee breaks/intervals
- As an introductory 'bang'
- To create specific atmospheres for special messages (film music, theme tunes, sound effects etc)
- To illustrate a point amusingly with a song 'snippet' (example for a presentation on customer service: 'Help', 'Keep the customer satisfied', 'You can't always get what you want' etc). Use 'oldies but goodies', to appeal to a majority

NB You can either take your MP3 player and speakers to the conference room, **or** incorporate the sound bites in your PowerPoint presentation (see page 63) **or** simply use your laptop as a music centre.

## SUPPORTING YOUR PRESENTATION

# H : THE CD/MP3 PLAYER

### RECORDED SPEECH

Recorded speech can be useful for:

- Illustrating messages (salesman-customer, boss-subordinate)
- Examples of opinions (market research interviews etc)
- Bringing an absent colleague to the presentation
- Interjecting humorous anecdotes
- Giving examples of current radio adverts/trends

Why not record your presentations so you can work on your mistakes?

> **Tip** *When recording audio examples, make sure you leave very little space between each recording. In this way you can press the 'pause' button at the end of one example, knowing that the next recording is cued to start as soon as you next hit the button.*

SUPPORTING YOUR PRESENTATION

# F : ANECDOTES AND METAPHORS

'F' is for Feelings and sensations! 42% of people say that their memories favour this kind of information and, when tested, the same people remember 80% of facts given while 'appealing to feeling' the previous day.

- **ANECDOTES** are true stories which give 'live' examples of what's being presented and help people remember the message. For instance:
    - 'I recall we had one manager who…'
    - 'Someone was working with this software last week and…'

- **METAPHORS** are comparisons/analogies/similes which illustrate what is being presented by comparing it to something very visual or more easily recognisable/understood. They usually start with the phrase, 'It's a bit like…'

    **Example**: the financial controller's sonar on page 60

## SUPPORTING YOUR PRESENTATION

# F : PARABLES

Parables persuade! They take away the defensive
reaction we tend to provoke in participants when we
ask them to change the way they do things.
Parables (like the 'Prodigal Son') refer to a third
party in a 'far away' place and thus feel safe.
The participant, nevertheless, connects
with the message and projects it onto
him/herself which allows SELF-
INITIATED change to take place.

You'll find a modern-day parable
on page 85 (The Story of Max).
Being aware of the fact that it's
trying to persuade you to
change, might make you feel
defensive. On the other hand,
maybe…

# F : TOUCH, TASTE AND SMELL

### TOUCH
Your audience will remember your key points much more clearly if they are INVOLVED. One way to ensure involvement is to give them something to touch. Handouts, samples, models, free gifts – all will help participants to participate and, therefore, remember.

### TASTE AND SMELL
On the face of it, it would seem highly inappropriate for you, as a presenter, to ask your audience to taste or smell something! But… think about candy and air fresheners which could simply lend atmosphere to your presentation and maybe even help link your message to something pleasant in the participants' minds. Even if you don't actually produce smoke in your 'Fire Hazards' presentation or give them some coffee in your 'HR Services' speech, you can always DESCRIBE tastes and smells!

## SUPPORTING YOUR PRESENTATION

# F : CROSS-SENSING

If you'd like to hypnotise your audience, do some 'cross-sensing'! This simply means describing something in a way which appeals to all the senses: SIGHT, HEARING, TOUCH, TASTE, SMELL, HEAT/COLD/PAIN/EMOTIONS.

A manager for a large multinational held her sales audience spellbound for 10 minutes as she described how a magnetic resonance scanner worked by taking them into a hospital in their minds. Some participants reported that they were actually able to feel what it was like to be inside the scanner.

# MURPHY'S LAW

**'If something can go wrong – it will!'**

O'Connor's corollary:
'Murphy was an optimist!'

The only way to beat Murphy
is to be a professional and
use the 3 P's:

- **Preparation**
- **Preparation**
- **Preparation**

# VIDEO FEEDBACK

Here's an idea to help you accelerate
your improvement as a presenter!

Film yourself at one of your next
presentations (remember to ask
the audience's permission) and
then play the tape back at home.

Give yourself:

- Five objectives to work on
  for your NEXT
  presentation

Did I say that?

**The Story of Max**

A PRESENTATIONS PARABLE

Maximilian Jones and the adventure

of the lost slides

# The Story of Max

Maximilian Jones is the well-meaning Finance Director of a medium-sized company. He's about your age but dresses a little more conservatively than you would if you had his position.

We meet Max as his wife drops him at the airport. He's off to Switzerland for the company's annual management conference and, what's more, the President has asked him to make a presentation.

*'Give 'em the good news and the bad, Max,'* he'd said two months previously, as they came out of the weekly review meeting. *'We did pretty well last year but we can't be getting complacent, so I want you to make it clear that we'll be keeping an eye on costs. Oh, and by the way, this year's conference will be in Davos. Got to keep the troops motivated, eh ? You do a bit of skiing Max, don't you?'*

Since then, of course, Max has been busy preparing. Max is a worrier and he's spent hours of nervous, painstaking work piecing together his 45-minute talk. Now, Max isn't what you'd call the world's best public speaker but, to be fair, he's not much worse than the rest of his colleagues who are on the programme.

Actually, in some ways he's better. He really does his homework. You see, he's frightened that the audience will be against him, watching his every move; out to trap him if he gets a figure wrong; analysing the soundness of every argument; judging him on the seriousness of his message.

So, he's prepared. Boy, is he prepared!

He's got a series of slides on discounted cash flow to show those HR boys that Finance is a serious business, a few product comparison graphs so Sales will know he's on top of things and ten or so charts on currency fluctuations for the last five years.

He secretly hopes they will be more accurate than the ones which Angus, the Treasurer, is bound to show!

His poor secretary was really glad to see him finally pack his laptop with the CD ROMs and the 43 back-up overhead slides into his suitcase and leave the office just before lunch this morning, but she didn't show it of course. *'Bye, Mr. Jones. We'll miss you. Enjoy the ski slopes, but be sure to wear your sun cream. Those rays can be wicked at that altitude, you know!'*

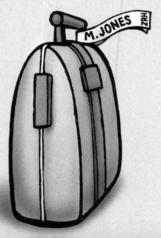

There's hardly any queue at the airport check-in counter and Max's baggage is handled by an efficient ground steward and whisked away in a flash. By the time Max gets to the gate and hands over his boarding card, there's an unaccustomed lightness to his step.

Max's neighbour on the flight is, as he discovers over a glass of white wine, a retired country doctor off to join his wife for a holiday at a friend's chalet near St. Moritz. Max tells him about the conference and the doctor seems interested.

'Well, I'm a bit nervous actually,' says Max, 'err ... I'll, um, be making a short slide presentation myself.'

'Slide?' asks the doctor, puzzled.

'Yes, you know, computer things. Visual aids on a big screen. All on memory sticks these days, of course. Need a backup on overhead transparencies though. Murphy's Law and all that!'

The doctor looks around to see where Max keeps these strange items.

'Ha. No, no,' says Max, pointing down to the plane's hold, 'got them in my suitcase!'

'Ah, right,' says the doctor, nodding, 'and err ... why are you making this ... um ... presentation?'

Max hesitates a moment before replying, as if he can't quite decide why it's such a good question.

'Why?'

'Yes,' repeats the doctor, 'why?'

'Well,' Max says slowly, *'I guess it's because our President is very keen on top-down communication.'*

*'Oh, really and … err … why's that?'*

Max is surprised at the doctor's insistence, a bit impatient with this old-fashioned, tweedy gentleman who's obviously so out of touch with the modern world.

*'Well, it's motivation, isn't it? I mean, keeping the troops informed helps motivate them.'*

The doctor smiles. *'Oh, I see, the people in your company are demotivated!'*

*'Oh, no, no, no,'* says Max quickly, *'quite the opposite actually. In fact, we did really well last year. Come to think of it, my little presentation will probably do more to demotivate them than anything else.'*

The doctor gives up, smiles, nods in a soothing sort of way and opens his 'Herald Tribune'.

Zurich airport is a model of clinical efficiency and minutes after landing Max is admiring the speed with which the bags have been rushed to the carousel.

Minutes later, however, he begins to panic.

The carousel has stopped turning, the
doctor has waved him a sympathetic
goodbye and all the other
passengers have left.

The airline has lost his suitcase with
all his slides for tomorrow's presentation!

The lady in the lost luggage office is
apologetic and businesslike. She has some
devastating news. They've traced Max's baggage and it's on the flight to Singapore. It won't
be back until the day after tomorrow at the earliest – but they'll send it by taxi to the hotel ...
of course.

Different people react differently under stress. Max is a fatalist and keeps his cool. Baggage-
less, he makes his way to the airport arrivals bar and orders a Feldschlösschen.

He is in deep trouble.

As he sips his beer he realises that there is no way he can even attempt to reproduce his presentation. He has no notes. Max's slides **are** his notes so he is totally lost without them. He's going to have to think fast. For some reason he first thinks back to the doctor on the plane. *'Why are you making this presentation?'*

*'Why, why, why?'* The words resonate in his head and Max thinks. He really thinks!

One hour and two beers later, Max gets up. He goes to the bank and gets some Swiss francs. He hurries to the chocolate shop, the paper store and the office supplies kiosk.

Then he hires a car and drives to the conference hotel. It's getting late when he arrives in Davos. The lights are coming on as he winds into the village, its roadsides deep with piled snow.

He checks into the hotel and immediately goes down to the hotel kitchen with a strange request. The Maitre d'Hotel humours him. *'Yes, of course, sir, we can get you two of those'*.

Max eats peanuts and Toblerone from the mini bar. He lies on the bed thinking. Max doesn't write any notes. It's too late. He watches a bit of CNN and thinks, *'I'm going to get fired for this'*.

Next morning Max goes down early. In the conference room there are five rows of ten tables; on each table are note pads with bright logos and gift pens. The chairs are comfortable and well-padded. There's no real stage but a small raised rostrum with a lectern and a table, a flip chart and an overhead projector. Max prepares. The LCD projector is set up at the back of the room. He won't be needing that! A banner to the side of the big screen proclaims, 'Winning Through Quality'.

The first part of the conference goes reasonably well. No surprises. The President's speech is, as expected, boring as hell and goes on far too long. Then comes the company's Legal Director with a totally incomprehensible review of forthcoming EU legislation. But he gets clapped at the end. Probably because he only ran over by 10 minutes.

And now it's Max's turn. Only 35 minutes left before the scheduled coffee break. The delegates are already yawning and stretching. Jerry Anderson is the HR Director and he's in the third row sitting next to the brand new Logistics Manager, Mary Griffiths. As Max walks glumly to the platform, Jerry looks at Mary and winks. *'This is going to be a laugh a minute,'* he says mischievously.

*'Ladies and gentlemen,'* says Max to the silent assembly, *'I have some good news and some ... err ... good news.'*

*'First, the good news. Last year, our company had a turnover of 200 million.'* Max ducks down behind the lectern and brings out an enormous glass salad bowl. Stuck on the back is a large piece of white card with TURNOVER written on it in big, bold letters. He places it carefully on the lectern and ducks down again to get what looks like a bulging pillow case tied with a rope.

*'200 million'*, he repeats opening the bag and pouring its contents into the bowl. Gold and silver chocolate coins, Swiss gold ingots and medals, and even a few real bank notes clatter and flutter into the glass bowl where they lie gleaming and glittering in the stage lights.

*'10 million of this was net profit and I'm here to tell you how we made so much,'* says Max, taking a large gold bar from the bowl and walking across to the table on the other side of the rostrum. He bends down under the table and presents the second salad bowl – this one with NET PROFIT written on its card. He carefully places the gold bar in the bowl.

*'I'm also here to describe three ways in which we can increase this 10 million to 13 million if we stop the ROT.'*

Max walks over to the flip chart and turns a page. There's a huge STOP sign drawn in the top right hand corner and the letters R O T down the left hand side of the sheet.

Jerry Anderson glances apprehensively at Mary, who seems to be mesmerised. *'Max has gone crazy,'* he thinks to himself. *'He's finally cracked under the pressure!'*

Max continues. *'Let me tell you why I think we did so well last year. First of all, Arthur and the R&D team gave us exactly the products which Rachel, in Market Research, had forecast the customers wanted.'*

*'John's Marketing group packaged and positioned them perfectly, which enabled Fred and the sales force to do such an outstanding job and come in at 125 per cent of quota!'*

Max notices the four of them smiling.

*'Maybe he's not so crazy,'* thinks Jerry, who's now also smiling.

Mary is still hypnotised.

*'So, that's the good news,'* says Max, getting into the swing of it, *'now for the ... um ... good news! As I said, if we can do three things even better, we can increase that ten million by another three.'*

Max walks over to the flip chart and, with a thick marker, completes the word RECEIVABLES after the R of ROT.

*'Outstanding days receivables are a great way of losing money! We often wait for over two months before we get paid for our excellent products! I mean, how would you feel if you had to wait for two months before we paid your salary?*

*'I know it's tough for the salesmen and women, Fred, but if we can stop allowing bad-paying customers 60 days to pay and cut payment terms to 30 days or less ... and Adrian, if we can send those bills out even one day earlier ... and Janet, if your team can talk nicely to some of our customers' accounts people when they slip behind with their payments ... then Angus, our beloved Treasurer, can put that money to work and earn up to one million more!'*

Max takes a big, gold coin from the TURNOVER bowl, carries it across to the table and drops it heavily into the NET PROFIT bowl.

'Now let's talk about 'O' for Office Supplies,' he says, writing it on the flip chart. 'It's amazing how much we waste. My team and I have made a list of every item we buy and there is an incredible amount of duplication, bad buying and slippage. Nothing dishonest, I assure you, but I guess, since it's not our money, we don't worry too much. Let me give you a couple of examples.'

Max pulls a CD ROM out of his pocket and holds it up.

'If we were to use these instead of the ones we currently buy, we'd save 30 per cent. Same quality, different supplier.'

He pauses, walks over to the table and picks up a pack of white envelopes.

'And you know something? We currently spend twice as much buying these white envelopes as does the prestigious Rolex watch company. Throwing money out of the window!'

A devilish, tempting thought crosses Max's mind like a lightning flash. He saw someone do it on television once and it worked. Dare he or dare he not? He takes a deep breath.

*'Yes,'* he repeats, *'throwing it out of the window!'*

And, with a sudden, baseball-type pitch, he hurls the envelopes out into the audience.

*'I was right first time,'* thinks Jerry, *'he has gone mad!'*

Grown men and women leap to their feet, laughing, to catch the falling envelopes. Mary holds one and grins at Jerry. Max can't believe his eyes. With an effort, he hides an impish smile.

*'All in all,'* he shouts above the general commotion, *'we could save at least another one million.'*

As the audience's attention returns, he takes another gold coin from the TURNOVER bowl over to the NET PROFIT bowl.

*'Thirdly'*, he announces dramatically, *'Travel Expenses!'*

Max writes the magic words after the big T on the flip chart as calm descends on the audience.

*'Now, I know, we all deserve this trip to Switzerland,'* he continues, *'and I wouldn't question the expense for one moment. But, back home, each of us is travelling constantly. Week in and week out – and we are clocking up an enormous travel bill. Think of your own travel schedule. When did you last take the train instead of buying a business class air ticket for what <u>looked</u> like a 45-minute trip which, in fact, took five hours door to door?'* (Max takes an air ticket from his jacket pocket and holds it above his head for a few seconds.)

*'Consider how much work you could get done on the train – in comfort and relative privacy. Hans, Rob, Angela ... I bet you could do with a couple more quiet hours a week away from the madding crowd! All of you, please think about what you would do if it were your own money.'*

'Did you know that a recent survey reported that 95 per cent of senior Swiss executives prefer to use the train for internal business trips even though flying is usually very dependable?'

This brings a few chuckles from those who have heard about Max's lost luggage.

'As from next month, we'll be asking you to fly Economy within Europe (like just about every other company I know), to take first class train trips whenever possible and keep taxi journeys to the minimum.'

'And, you've guessed it, this will bring in at least another one million!' The last gold coin tumbles into the NET PROFIT bowl which Max picks up and carries forward to the front of the rostrum.

'Ladies and gentlemen, these three million are yours if you will help me stop the ROT by controlling Receivables, Offices Supplies and Travel Expenses.'

*'I've decided that in a couple of weeks you'll all be receiving a little booklet based on this presentation. I'm going to call it '101 ways to save money'. And you'll see, stopping the ROT covers only a few. There are many, many more!'*

Jerry looks at his watch. *'My God,'* he thinks, *'he's finished and it only took 10 minutes.'*

As if he'd heard him, Max finalises. *'This is your money,'* he says holding the bow out towards the audience, *'but I'm now going to give it to Angus, our dear Treasurer, for safe keeping. Knowing him, he'll make it into 14 million! I apologise for giving you 20 minutes extra coffee break, but that's all I really wanted to talk about. Thank you!'*

In a daze, Max steps down from the platform and hands the bowl to a smiling Angus. The room breaks into spontaneous applause and cheering led by Mary who can't take her eyes off the tired, sheepish-looking Max as the President strides forward and slaps him on the back.

*'Max,'* he beams, *'that was superb. Didn't know you had it in you. Best presentation I've ever heard you make! Wonderful! Now come and have a coffee. I'd like you to talk me through that budget proposal for your department again.'* He guides Max towards the foyer.

As the audience follow them out, Jerry looks at Mary: *'I guess that's what happens when you lose your slides,'* he chuckles and shrugs his shoulders.

**NOTES**

# PRESENTATION CHECKLIST

**PRESENTATION CHECKLIST**

# DISPROVING MURPHY'S LAW

'If something can go wrong – it will!'

or, as Robert Burns said:

'The best-laid schemes o' mice an' men gang aft agley.'

In order to try and disprove Murphy's law next time you have to make a presentation, make sure you:

- Use a presentation checklist
- Go to the conference room the day before the presentation and go through your checklist; make sure you talk to someone responsible about missing items
- Go to the conference room again at least 30 minutes before the start of the morning/afternoon session when you are on and go through everything once again

If it's good enough for Lufthansa, it's good enough for you!

# PRESENTATION CHECKLIST

| PRESENTATION | ① ✓ | ② ✓ | NOTES |
|---|---|---|---|
| Presentation notes | | | |
| PowerPoint Slides/CD/Stick | | | |
| Laptop | | | |
| Music CD's/MP3 | | | |
| Handouts | | | |
| Gimmicks | | | |

# PRESENTATION CHECKLIST

| ACCESSORIES | ① | ② | NOTES |
|---|---|---|---|
| Laser pointer | | | |
| Felt tip markers | | | |
| Masking tape | | | |
| Penknife/screwdriver | | | |
| Spare flip chart paper | | | |
| Plugs/leads | | | |

# PRESENTATION CHECKLIST

| A/V EQUIPMENT | ① ✓ | ② ✓ | NOTES |
|---|---|---|---|
| Beamer | | | |
| Flip chart | | | |
| Screen | | | |
| Whiteboard/pinboard | | | |
| Remote controls? | | | |
| CD/MP3 player | | | |
| Video/DVD equipment | | | |
| Amplifier/speakers | | | |
| Microphone | | | |

## About the Author

**John Townsend, BA MA MCIPD**
John has built a reputation internationally as a leading trainer of
trainers. He is the founder of the highly-regarded Master Trainer
Institute, a total learning facility located just outside Geneva which
draws trainers and facilitators from around the world. He set up
the Institute after 30 years' experience in international consulting
and human resource management positions in the UK, France,
the United States and Switzerland.

From 1978–1984 he was European Director of Executive
Development with GTE in Geneva with training responsibility for over
800 managers in some 15 countries.  John has published a number of
management and professional guides and regularly contributes articles
to leading management and training journals.

Many thanks to Richard Bradley of The Master Training Institute for helping these tips and
techniques come alive in Train the Trainer courses for participants from all over the world.
You can contact Richard at: richard@mastertrainer.ch or www.mt-institute.com

**Contact:**
John Townsend, The Master Trainer Institute,
L'Avant Centre, 13 chemin du Levant, Ferney-Voltaire, France
Tel: (33) 450 42 84 16    Fax: (33) 450 40 57 37    www.mt-institute.com

# ORDER FORM

### Your details

Name _____

Position _____

Company _____

Address _____

_____

_____

Telephone _____

Fax _____

E-mail _____

VAT No. (EC companies) _____

Your Order Ref _____

### Please send me:

| | | No. copies |
|---|---|---|
| The Presentations Pocketbook | | |
| The _____ Pocketbook | | |
| The _____ Pocketbook | | |
| The _____ Pocketbook | | |

### Order by Post
**MANAGEMENT POCKETBOOKS LTD**
LAUREL HOUSE, STATION APPROACH,
ALRESFORD, HAMPSHIRE SO24 9JH UK

### Order by Phone, Fax or Internet
Telephone: +44 (0)1962 735573
Facsimile: +44 (0)1962 733637
E-mail: sales@pocketbook.co.uk
Web: www.pocketbook.co.uk

*Customers in USA should contact:*
**Management Pocketbooks**
2427 Bond Street, University Park, IL 60466
Telephone: 866 620 6944  Facsimile: 708 534 7803
E-mail: mp.orders@ware-pak.com
Web: www.managementpocketbooks.com

# THE MANAGEMENT POCKETBOOK SERIES

## Pocketbooks (also available in e-book format)

360 Degree Feedback
Absence Management
Appraisals
Assertiveness
Balance Sheet
Business Planning
Business Writing
Call Centre Customer Care
Career Transition
Coaching
Communicator's
Competencies
Creative Manager's
C.R.M.
Cross-cultural Business
Customer Service
Decision-making
Delegation
Developing People
Diversity
Emotional Intelligence
Employment Law
Empowerment
Energy and Well-being
Facilitator's
Flexible Workplace

Handling Complaints
Icebreakers
Impact & Presence
Improving Efficiency
Improving Profitability
Induction
Influencing
International Trade
Interviewer's
I.T. Trainer's
Key Account Manager's
Leadership
Learner's
Management Models
Manager's
Managing Assessment Centres
Managing Budgets
Managing Cashflow
Managing Change
Managing Customer Service
Managing Difficult Participants
Managing Recruitment
Managing Upwards
Managing Your Appraisal
Marketing
Meetings

Mentoring
Motivation
Negotiator's
Networking
NLP
Nurturing Innovation
Openers & Closers
People Manager's
Performance Management
Personal Success
Positive Mental Attitude
Presentations
Problem Behaviour
Problem Solving
Project Management
Psychometric Testing
Resolving Conflict
Reward
Sales Excellence
Salesperson's
Self-managed Development
Starting In Management
Strategy
Stress
Succeeding at Interviews
Tackling Difficult Conversations

Talent Management
Teambuilding Activities
Teamworking
Telephone Skills
Telesales
Thinker's
Time Management
Trainer Standards
Trainer's
Training Evaluation
Training Needs Analysis
Virtual Teams
Vocal Skills
Working Relationships
Workplace Politics

### Pocketfiles

Trainer's Blue Pocketfile of
Ready-to-use Activities

Trainer's Green Pocketfile of
Ready-to-use Activities

Trainer's Red Pocketfile of
Ready-to-use Activities

09.09